KEV's QuickStart.
FINGERSTYLE
Ukulele 2

T0088820

A QuickStart™ Ukulele Method book
BY KEV-KEVIN RONES

To access audio files for this book visit:
www.HalLeonard.com/QuickStartLessonsLibrary

Enter Code
8121-4264-8628-0385

Cover Design, Illustration, Book Design, Layout & Production, Original Music, Musical Arrangements,
Audio Recordings and Teaching Method by KEV-Kevin Rones

Kev's QuickStart™ & Kev's Learn & Play™

ISBN is 978- 1- 57424-369-7

Copyright © 2018 CENTERSTREAM Publishing
P.O. Box 17878 - Anaheim Hills, CA 92817

Phone: 714-779-9390 www.centerstream-usa.com

WELCOME! ABOUT THIS BOOK.

This book was written as a follow-up to the *QuickStart™ Fingerstyle Ukulele Book*. The arrangements in this book will introduce you to a variety of fingerstyle techniques that will help you improve your ukulele playing. You should have a basic understanding of how to read ukulele tablature (TAB) and know some basic ukulele fundamentals.

ABOUT THE TUNES IN THIS BOOK

The purpose of this book is to teach you a variety of fingerpicking techniques that you can put into your ukulele toolbox and use in your repertoire to enhance your playing ability and increase your skill level.

This is NOT a songbook. Each Exersong™ in this book was created to help you develop fingerstyle techniques. Pieces are intentionally short so you can understand the techniques and try them over and over without having to play through pages of music. The recordings for this book are designed to be used as learning tools. They are intentionally recorded at slower tempos without embellishments to help you learn the techniques.

LOW G -VS- HIGH G STRINGS

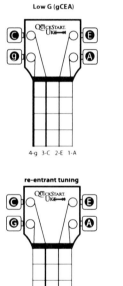

Most ukuleles come out of the box with a High G string tuned to Standard C6 Ukulele Tuning (GCEA).
In the last decade the ukulele has become increasingly popular with performers and songwriters. For songwriters, fingerstyle players, jazz players, classical players, and blues players the *Low G string* has gained overwhelming popularity.

The ExerSongs™ in this book were voiced for ukuleles strung with a *Low G ukulele string (gCEA).* You can play all the arrangements in the book using a ukulele strung with a *High G string*; however we recommend changing your **G** (4) string to a *Low G string* to add the additional lower bass notes not available in *High G strung* ukuleles. Most music stores can help you change out your *High G string* for a *Low G string*.

To access audio files for Fingerstyle Ukulele 2 visit: **www.HalLeonard.com/QuickStartLessonsLibrary**
and enter the code printed on the title page of this book

EXERSONGS™

LESSONS

BASIC FINGERSTYLE TECHNIQUES

THE PULL-OFF

1. Place both fingers on the fretboard
2. Anchor the Index fingers
3. Pull your middle finger off the string toward your palm to create the sound of the second note

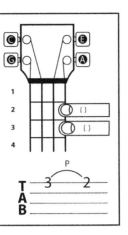

The **Pull-off** is a common technique used in Fingerstyle Ukulele. *Pull-offs* are created by plucking a fretted note and pulling your finger off the fretboard toward your palm to reveal the note below it. You get two notes for the price of one pluck!

In the example *Pull-off* we start in **Second Position** with the *index* anchored on the second fret and the *middle finger* fretting the third fret. With both fingers down, strike the string and pull your middle finger off the fretboard in a downward motion toward your palm. You should get two distinct notes with one pluck.

To do the Hammer-on example start in **Second Position** with the *index* anchored on the second fret. Then strike the string and "***hammer down***" your *middle finger* onto the third fret to create the second note. *Two distinct notes for the price of one hammer.*

A TIP FOR PLAYING HAMMER-ONS

Pluck the string more forcefully before the **Hammer-on** so the string is vibrating when the hammer occurs. Hammer your finger quickly and keep the "Hammer" down until the note rings out.

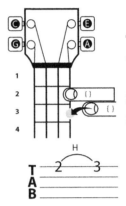

THE HAMMER-ON

1. Anchor your *index finger* on the second fret
2. Strike the string
3. Hammer down with your middle finger to create the sound of the second note

WHY DO PULL-OFFS AND HAMMER-ONS LOOK THE SAME?

The **Hammer-on** looks similar to a *Pull-off*. The Hammer-on technique is used when going from a lower pitch to a Higher Pitch. A *Pull-off* is used when going from a higher pitch to a lower pitch. Depending on the software used the notation for *Pull-offs* and *Hammer-ons* varies.

Occasionally you might see **Pull-offs** indicated with the letters **P.O.** above the arc.

Hammer-ons are sometimes indicated similarly with the letters **H.O.** above the arc.

When there are no letters above the arc in the notation use common sense to determine if it's a *Hammer-on* (lower note to higher note) or a *Pull-off* (higher note to lower note).

3 WAYS PULL-OFFS ARE NOTATED

3 WAYS HAMMER-ONS ARE NOTATED

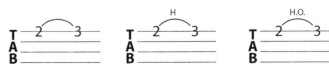

WHAT IS THE DIFFERENCE BETWEEN A SLUR, A SHIFT SLIDE AND A LEGATO SLIDE?

When referring to playing the ukulele the term **Slur** means to slide from one pitch to another smoothly without stopping. All slides could be considered to be *Slurs*. We generally just use the generic term **Slide** since it better explains the technique.

There are two common types of slides: The **Shift Slide** and the **Legato Slide**.

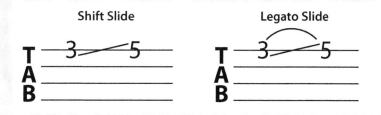

A **Shift Slide** is technically done by striking the first note of the slide and then also striking the ending note of the slide. You hear two distinct notes. This technique is less commonly used.

Legato Slur (formerly just called a **Slide**) is a fairly new term used to describe a common slide where you pluck the note once and slide to the next note. *Legato* is Italian for *tied together*.
Most players consider this technique the defacto slide. What confuses people is the way it is notated.

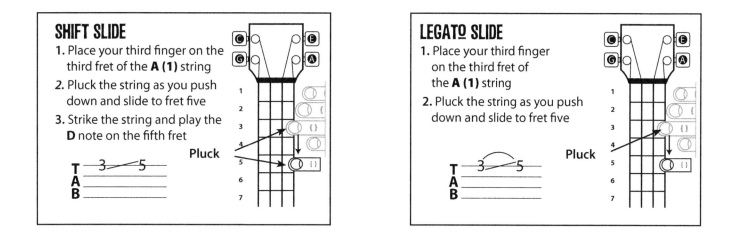

SHIFT SLIDE

1. Place your third finger on the third fret of the **A (1)** string
2. Pluck the string as you push down and slide to fret five
3. Strike the string and play the **D** note on the fifth fret

Pluck

LEGATO SLIDE

1. Place your third finger on the third fret of the **A (1)** string
2. Pluck the string as you push down and slide to fret five

Pluck

FOR THIS BOOK....

Because of the limitations of some notation methods and the more recent adoption of the *Legato Slur* notation, the *Shift Slide* notation is commonly 'assumed' to represent the *Legato* technique.
The *Basic Slide* is almost always done **Legato** - with only one note plucked.
For this book we will assume all slides are played as *Legato Slides*.

HOW DO YOU KNOW WHICH FINGERS TO PICK WITH?

Lesson: Understanding Right Hand pima Picking Notation

Each of our hands has a different nomenclature for identifying the fingers in music notation.

The **right hand** (picking hand) fingers are identified by the **pima** system. It is used to clarify right hand picking and can be found next to the note, or above or below the music or tablature. The **pima** system uses lower case letters: (**p**) for *thumb*, (**i**) for *index*, (**m**) for middle and (**a**) for the ring finger. We very rarely use the right hand pinky. In some Classical or Flamenco notation the pinky is noted as (**c**), (**x**) or (**e**).

In the first measure of *"There And Back Again"*you can see the right hand **pima** fingering in the music notation. The fingering for the picking pattern is written in the first measure and repeated for the entire piece. Throughout this book you will see right hand fingerings indicated by **pima** notation where needed.

Right
Picking Hand

The fingers of the *Fretting hand* (left) are named :
T for *thumb*
1 for *index*
2 for *middle*
3 for the *ring* finger and
4 for the *pinky*

We use these numbers on *Chord Diagrams* to show recommended chord fingerings

F

2 0 1 0

Left
Fretting Hand

In the Exersong™ *There and Back Again* the **Tempo** and the **Picking** pattern remain the same through the entire piece. *All you have to do is change chords!*

F   A   B♭   B♭m   C   C7

2 0 1 0   2 1 0 0   3 2 1 1   3 1 1 1   0 0 0 3   0 0 0 1

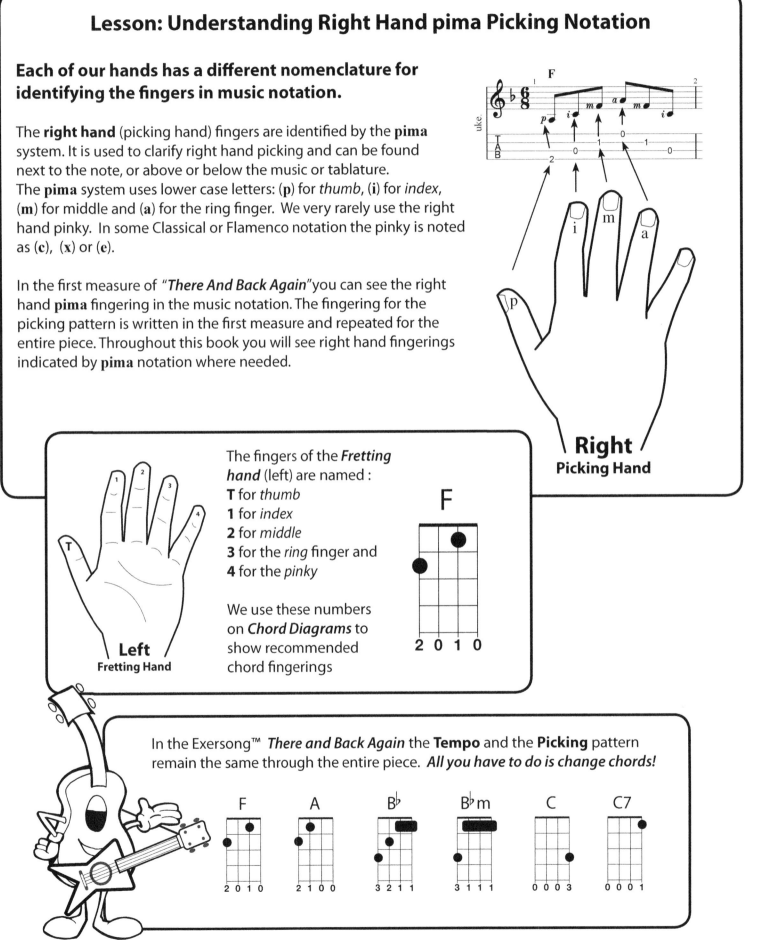

There And Back Again

Music by KEV

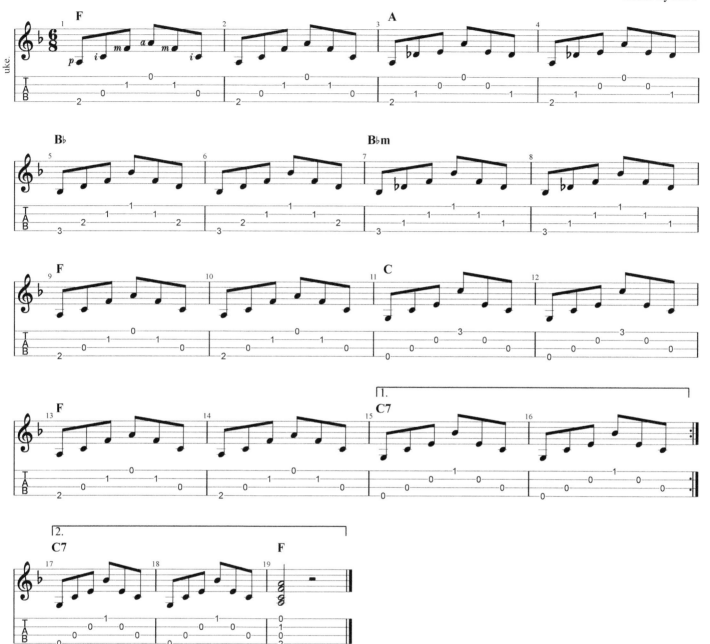

Performance notes:

Play each note using the **right** (picking) hand **pima** system. This exersong™ is in 6/8 time. That means you can count 6 eighth notes per measure. Learn the chords first. The pattern repeats throughout this piece. The key to playing fingerstyle picking patterns smoothly is to know the pattern, be able to switch your chords and to practice it slowly and precisely. Make sure there is equal space between each plucked note and do not pause between chords.

Study: Ascending Bass line

Original

Music by KEV

Lesson: Playing an Ascending Bass Line

The Two Note Pinch

If you look at the **pima** notation over first notes in the first measure of this piece you will see $\frac{m}{p}$. This means you pluck the *thumb* (p) on the fourth string at the same time as you play the middle finger (**m**) of the first string. Pinch the two strings with a slight pressure and pull them off at the same time. *mf* is a dynamic notation standing for **mezzo-forte**, meaning "Moderately loud." Not to be confused with right hand **pima** notation.

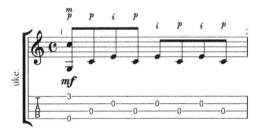

The Double Thumb Technique

In this piece we use a double thumb technique in the picking pattern. Look at the **pima** notation above the first measure and you will the see that it indicates a *thumb/middle* (**p/m**) pinch followed by: *thumb* (**p**) *index* (**i**), *thumb* (**p**) *index* (**i**), *thumb* (**p**) *index* (**i**), *thumb* (**p**). This is the double thumb technique.

Performance notes:

Often in fingerstyle we will do variations of the picking pattern to include melody notes - or to make certain notes in a chord more prominent. In measures 4 and 7 the picking pattern varies. After you get more experience playing fingerstyle pieces you will begin to recognize the picking patterns that work best over certain chords.

Study: Descending Bass Line

Original

Music by KEV

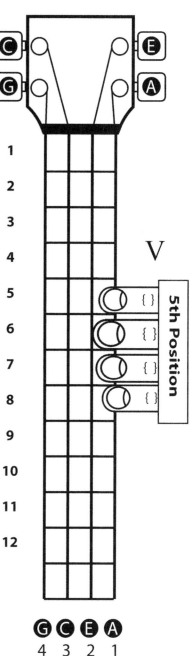

Lesson: Playing a Descending Bass Line

Playing In Position

If you watch good musicians they seem to play effortlessly up and down the neck. They can do this because they have learned the concept of **"Playing In Position."** Position is determined by where you place your left hand on the fretboard. Your index finger determines the name of the position.

Position is noted with **Roman Numerals**. If you look above the first measure of the piece you will see the **Roman Numeral** V. This tells you to move your hand so the *index* finger is over the fifth fret. You will see *Roman Numeral Position Markers* throughout the pieces in this book. Always move your index to the fret number indicated by the **Roman Numeral**.

Performance notes:

Pay attention to the Roman Numeral position markers and move your hand to the correct fret. Use the double thumb technique and pay attention to the picking pattern and the right (picking) hand **pima** notations .

M.Carcassi Opus 6 No. 7

Traditional

Arranged By KEV

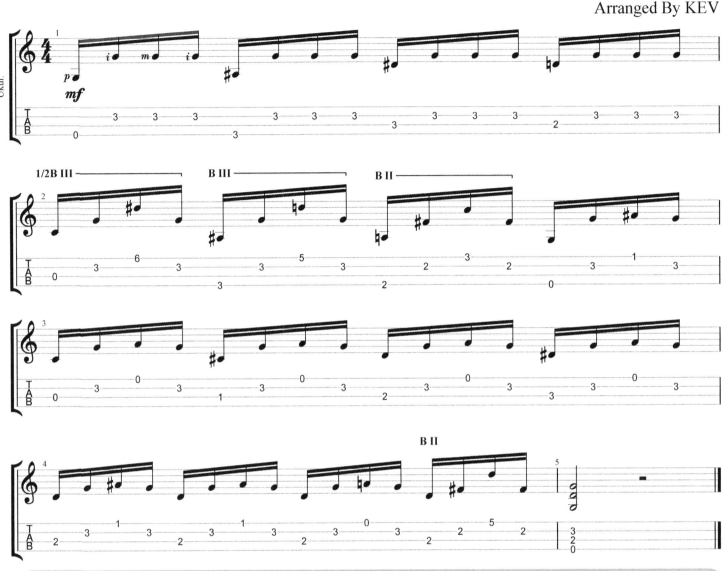

Matteo Carcassi (1792 – 16 January 1853) **was a well known Italian guitarist and composer.**
He wrote a method for guitar that included collected works from his time. The Carcassi classical guitar
studies are still popular today. .

Performance notes:

Use the right hand "Walking Fingers" picking technique. Be aware of the *Barre* indicators. In the first measure
start by anchoring your left hand *ring* finger (3) on the **G** note located on the third fret of string 2.
Use your *thumb* (**p**) to strike the bass notes on strings 3 and 4, and alternate the *index* (**i**) and *middle* (**m**).
Practice slowly and precisely. Count out loud and tap your foot on the downbeat of each 16th note grouping.
There should be equal space between each note.

A GENERAL RULE OF FINGERPICKING

The right hand picking thumb (**p**) is generally used on strings 4 (**G**) and 3 (**C**). The right
hand (picking) *index* finger is assigned string 2 (**E**) and the *middle* finger is used on
string 1 (**A**). With this technique the *thumb* has more weight in the downward motion
on strings 3 & 4, which is often preferred in fingerstyle playing.

Lesson: Walking Fingers - Alternating Index and Middle Finger Picking Technique

This piece uses a thumb strike of the bass note and an alternating *index* (**i**) and *middle* (**m**) finger technique. If you are using proper form the right hand thumb is in front of the other fingers. The thumb pushes down and the fingers pluck upward. In each grouping of sixteenth notes you will use your thumb (**p**) on the first note and alternate *index* (**i**) *middle* (**m**) and *index* (**i**).

Understanding Barre or Capo indicators

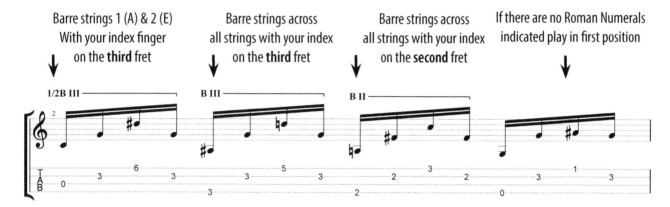

The term **Barre** means to use one finger to bar across more than one string at a time. Unless otherwise indicated the Barre is done with the *index* (1) finger of your fretting hands. In this book the Barre is indicated by a capitol **B** followed by roman numerals, which tell you what fret to **Barre** across. 1/2 B III indicates you *Barre half the strings* **A (1)** and **E (2)** with your index finger. B III tells you to Barre across *all four strings* on the third fret. The term "Capo" is used in some notation. **Capo III or CIII** generally means to use a device (the Capo) to clamp onto or wrap around the fretboard at the third fret raising the pitch.

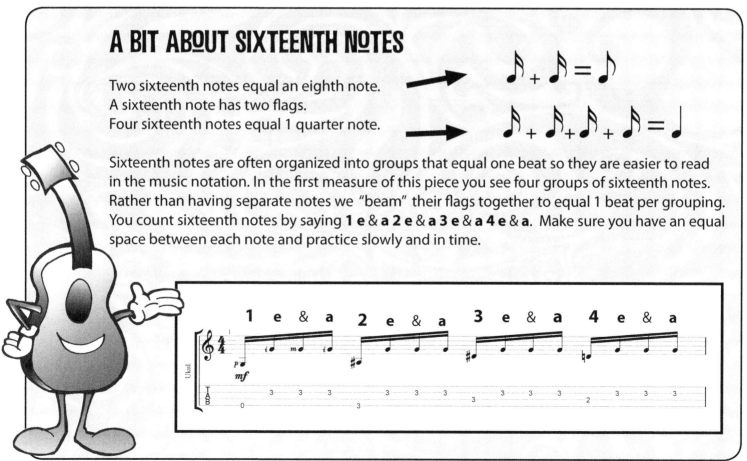

A BIT ABOUT SIXTEENTH NOTES

Two sixteenth notes equal an eighth note.
A sixteenth note has two flags.
Four sixteenth notes equal 1 quarter note.

Sixteenth notes are often organized into groups that equal one beat so they are easier to read in the music notation. In the first measure of this piece you see four groups of sixteenth notes. Rather than having separate notes we "beam" their flags together to equal 1 beat per grouping. You count sixteenth notes by saying **1 e & a 2 e & a 3 e & a 4 e & a**. Make sure you have an equal space between each note and practice slowly and in time.

Malagueña

Traditional

Arranged by KEV

"Malagueña" is a song by Cuban composer Ernesto Lecuona. Written in 1928, it was originally the sixth movement of Lecuona's Suite Andalucia, to which he added lyrics in Spanish. The form of the song was adopted by Flamenco and Classical guitarists and has evolved into a variety of improvised styles. It was made popular by Andrés Segovia and Flamenco sensation Sabicas in the 1950s.

Lesson: Malagueña with Peddle Tone Kicker Technique and a Rasgueado

Peddle Tones

In *measures 1-4* of this piece we use only the thumb to strike the strings. In *measures 5-8* we incorporate a peddle tone kicker. A peddle tone is a **repeating note that is played with a melody**. In this exersong™ the peddle tone is the first string (**A**). Play the peddle tone using your middle finger (**m**) in an upward "kicking " motion after every downward thumb strike.

The Rasgueado Technique

The **Rasgueado** (rozz•key•ah•though) is a Flamenco technique. It roughly translates to mean "fan" technique. A true Rasgueado contains 5 strums in a single beat. This is done by fanning your right hand fingers across the strings *pinky* first, then *ring*, then *middle*, then index and then doing an upstroke with the *index* finger… all in one beat! Since most beginners cannot do this technique we use a modified version of the *Rasgueado* by simply fanning your *ring*, *middle* and *index* fingers across the strings.

If you look at **Section B**, measure 9 you will see the word **rasg**. This is the musical notation for the *Rasgueado* or "*fan*" technique. In this instance you would form an **A** Chord and do the *Rasgueado* fan technique.

Performance notes:

Remember to strike down with the flesh of the left side of your thumb and to kick up with your *middle* finger on the first string. Use a rocking motion downward and upward alternating between the downward thumb strike and the upward middle finger kicker. Space the notes evenly! Try to play the simple rasgueado until you can develop the skill to do a true five beat rasgueado.

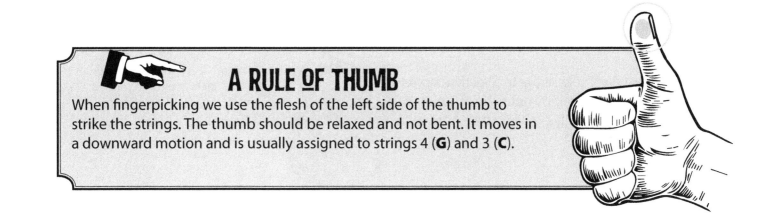

A RULE OF THUMB

When fingerpicking we use the flesh of the left side of the thumb to strike the strings. The thumb should be relaxed and not bent. It moves in a downward motion and is usually assigned to strings 4 (**G**) and 3 (**C**).

The Streets Of Laredo
Traditional

Arranged By KEV

> **"The Streets of Laredo",** also known as the **"Cowboy's Lament"**, is a famous American cowboy ballad derived from the English folk song **"The Unfortunate Rake"**. The title refers to the city of Laredo, Texas.

Lesson : Chords with Melody

The Chord Pull Technique

The **"Chord Pull"** technique is done by grabbing all four strings at the same time with your picking hand, squeezing slightly downward with the thumb and upward with the fingers (**i, m, a**). Rather than strum the strings, slightly "pull" all four strings upward and release them at the same time.

By *"pulling"* the chord we can control its *attack* and *decay*. It also allows us to give more emphasis to the melody note when chords are combined with a series of melody notes that are played as musical phrases.

Performance notes:

Use the **"Chord Pull"** technique to play the chords. In this exersong™ the melody note is incorporated into chords. Play smoothly between the chord pulls and the melody notes.

IMPORTANT!
USE PROPER TECHNIQUE
When playing Fingerstyle Ukulele the picking hand thumb should be above the fingers as demonstrated in the image above. We use this hand position for all picking and strumming.

Santa Lucia

Traditional

"*Santa Lucia*" is a traditional Neapolitan song. It was translated by Teodoro Cottrau (1827–1879) into Italian and published by the Cottrau firm as a "barcarolla" or traditional folk song sung by Venetian gondoliers in Naples.

The original lyrics of "Santa Lucia" describe the picturesque waterfront district Borgo Santa Lucia in the Bay of Naples, and the invitation of a boatman to take a turn in his boat, to better enjoy the beauty and cool of the evening.

Lesson : Playing under the Barre

Barre across the fifth fret & hold it down until the last note indicated is played.

In *measures 9* and *10* of this exersong™ you can see a *Barre indicator* with an extended line. This tells us to hold the barrre for the duration of the notes under the extended line.

Performance notes:

Pay attention to the **Roman Numerals** and move your hand position to the correct fret. Hold the *Barre* down and play the notes under the Barre as indicated by the *Barre line extension*.

Ah! Vous Dirai-Je, Maman Variation #1

Traditional

Arranged by KEV

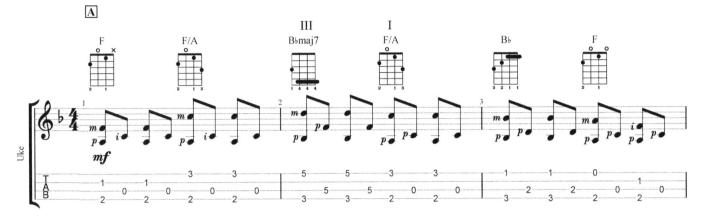

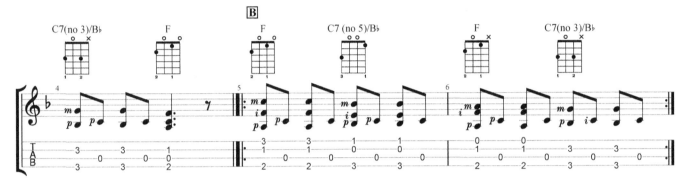

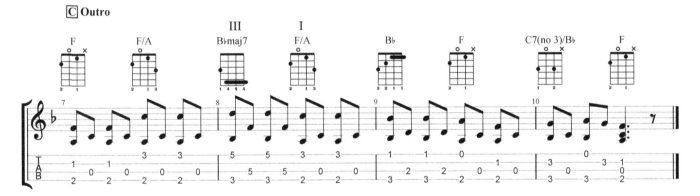

You might recognize this melody as the classic children's song **"Twinkle Twinkle Little Star."**
It is sung to the tune of the French melody **"Ah! vous dirai-je, maman"**, which translates roughly to
"Ah, would I tell you, Mom."
This was first published in 1761 and later arranged by several composers including Mozart in his
Twelve Variations of "Ah vous dirai-je, Maman." The English lyrics were first published in 1806 by Jane
Taylor with the title **"The Star"** in **Rhymes for the Nursery** by Jane and her sister, Ann Taylor.

Lesson : Two Finger Pluck with an Index Kicker

Plucking Technique:

Use your *thumb* (**p**) and *middle* finger (**m**) to pluck 2 strings at once. Create a peddle tone by using your *index* finger to strike the third string (**C**) after every two-string pluck. Count out loud as you pluck each set of notes in the measure: 1 & 2 & 3 & 4 & . Each time you say the word "and" you should be striking upward with your *index* (**i**) finger.

Performance notes:

Think of a clock when you practice this piece. Make sure your timing is the same throughout the piece. In the second measure there is a shift to third position. Think of the notes as a chord shape and practice moving from first position to third position without missing a beat.

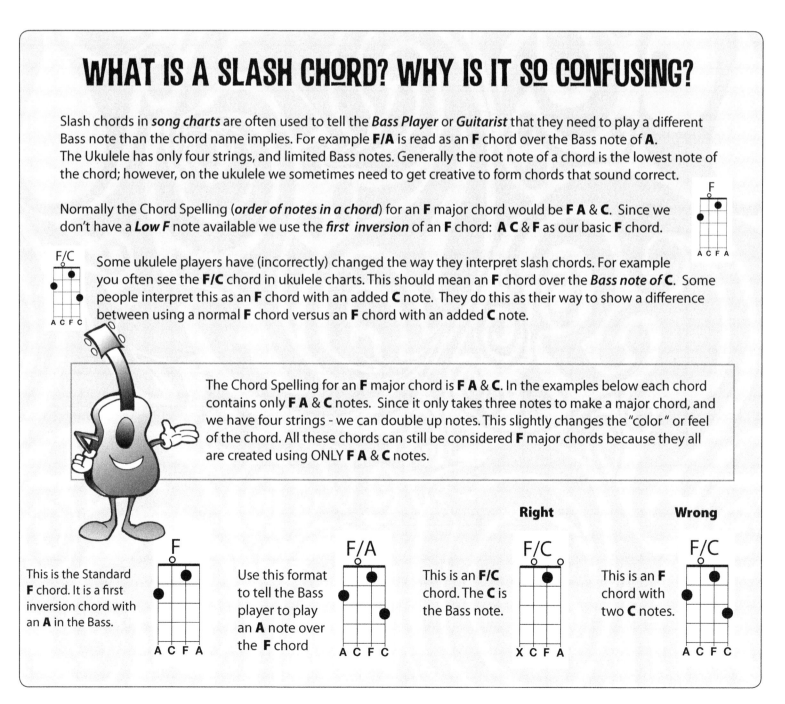

WHAT IS A SLASH CHORD? WHY IS IT SO CONFUSING?

Slash chords in *song charts* are often used to tell the *Bass Player* or *Guitarist* that they need to play a different Bass note than the chord name implies. For example **F/A** is read as an **F** chord over the Bass note of **A**. The Ukulele has only four strings, and limited Bass notes. Generally the root note of a chord is the lowest note of the chord; however, on the ukulele we sometimes need to get creative to form chords that sound correct.

Normally the Chord Spelling (*order of notes in a chord*) for an **F** major chord would be **F A** & **C**. Since we don't have a *Low F* note available we use the *first inversion* of an **F** chord: **A C** & **F** as our basic **F** chord.

Some ukulele players have (incorrectly) changed the way they interpret slash chords. For example you often see the **F/C** chord in ukulele charts. This should mean an **F** chord over the *Bass note of C*. Some people interpret this as an **F** chord with an added **C** note. They do this as their way to show a difference between using a normal **F** chord versus an **F** chord with an added **C** note.

The Chord Spelling for an **F** major chord is **F A** & **C**. In the examples below each chord contains only **F A** & **C** notes. Since it only takes three notes to make a major chord, and we have four strings - we can double up notes. This slightly changes the "color" or feel of the chord. All these chords can still be considered **F** major chords because they all are created using ONLY **F A** & **C** notes.

F

This is the Standard **F** chord. It is a first inversion chord with an **A** in the Bass.

F/A

Use this format to tell the Bass player to play an **A** note over the **F** chord

Right

F/C

This is an **F/C** chord. The **C** is the Bass note.

Wrong

F/C

This is an **F** chord with two **C** notes.

Cockles And Mussels (Molly Malone)

Traditional

Arrangement by KEV

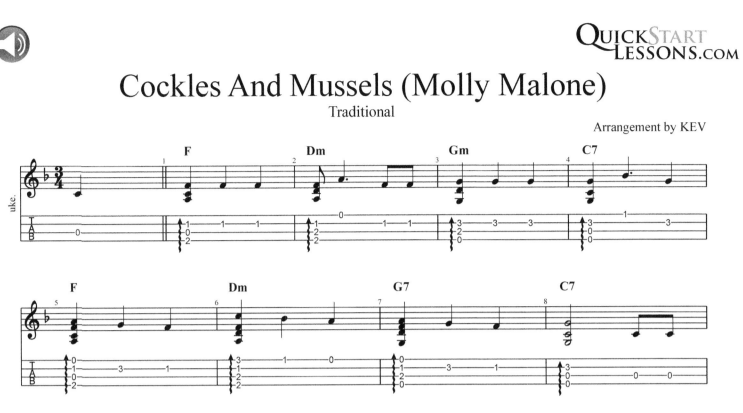

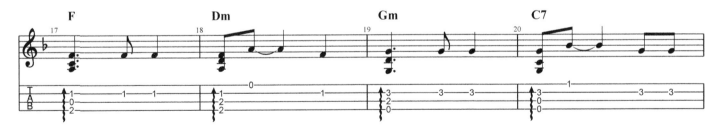

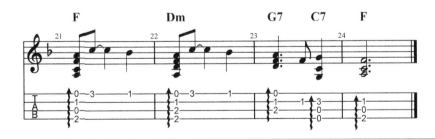

"Cockles and Mussels" (also known as *"Molly Malone"* or *"In Dublin's Fair City"*) is a popular song set in Dublin, Ireland, which has become the unofficial anthem of Dublin. The song tells a tragic tale of a woman in the late 20th century who sold fish and seafood on the streets of Dublin until she died at a young age of a fever.

Lesson: The Arpeggiation Technique

For this exercise we want to create a quick *"harp-like"* effect on the chords indicated with an arpeggio symbol. Look at the first chord in the piece. The symbol for Arpeggio is found in the tablature directly to the left of the the first **F** chord. It looks like a squiggly line with an arrow.

The arpeggio technique is played by placing your thumb on the top or fourth string (**G**), your *index* on the third string (**C**), your *middle* on the second string (**E**) and your *ring* finger on the first string (**A**).

The Arpeggio symbol

Remember when reading TAB the bottom line is the 4th string (**G**). In this example the *thumb* (**p**) plucks first, then the *index* on string 3 and the *middle* on string 2.

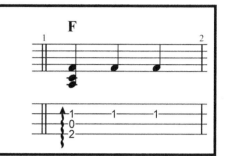

Your *thumb* should be placed so the left side of your thumb strikes the string. The other strings are held by your fingertips. If only three notes are indicated in the arpeggiated chord use the *thumb* (**p**), *middle* (**i**), and *ring* (a) fingers.

To *arpeggiate a chord* gently pluck the thumb downward and then turn your plucking hand palm upward allowing each finger to pull off the strings one at a time: *index* (**i**), *middle* (**m**) and *ring* (**a**). The trick is to pluck the thumb and play the remaining strings with equal space between the notes.

Performance notes:

Use the ***Arpeggio Technique*** to enhance and soften the chords of the song and make sure the emphasis is on the melody. Everything in this piece is done in first position.

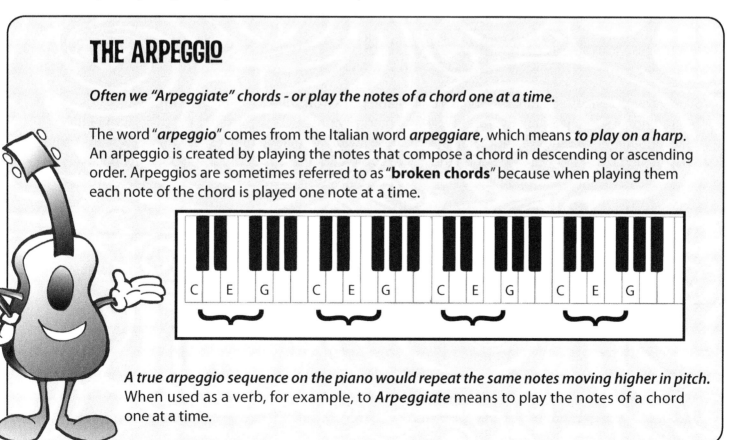

THE ARPEGGIO

Often we "Arpeggiate" chords - or play the notes of a chord one at a time.

The word *"arpeggio"* comes from the Italian word *arpeggiare*, which means ***to play on a harp***. An arpeggio is created by playing the notes that compose a chord in descending or ascending order. Arpeggios are sometimes referred to as **"broken chords"** because when playing them each note of the chord is played one note at a time.

A true arpeggio sequence on the piano would repeat the same notes moving higher in pitch. When used as a verb, for example, to **Arpeggiate** means to play the notes of a chord one at a time.

Scarborough Fair

Traditional

Arranged by KEV

"Scarborough Fair" is a traditional English ballad about the Yorkshire town of Scarborough. The traditional song lyrics tell the tale of a young man who instructs the listener to tell his former lover to perform for him a series of impossible tasks. These included making him a shirt without a seam and then washing it in a dry well. He added that if she completed these tasks he would take her back.

IS THERE AN EASIER WAY TO PLAY A BARRE CHORD?

The short answer is no. But the good news is you can use altered fingerings in some instances to make it easier. Here are two ways to play a **G/B** chord.

Lesson: Open & Closed Position Chords

We can use **Open** or **Closed position** chords on the Ukulele. An *Open Position* chord would be any chord that contains an *open* or non-fretted string.

A *Closed Position* chord would be any chord that has no open strings. *Closed Position Chords* are moveable shapes that can be moved up the neck to create other chords. In this piece we use *Closed Position* chords to play the melody higher up the neck while still maintaining the chord.

In *measure 6* we use a higher voicing of **Dm**, and in *measure 9* we use a higher voicing of **Bb** so we can "comp" the chord and play the melody note at the same time.

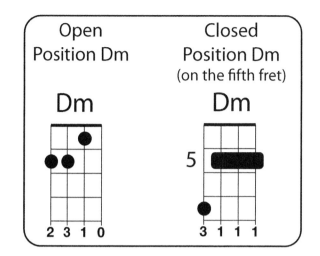

Performance notes:
This piece is in 3/4 time. Each measure gets three beats. Practice moving from the open chords to the closed position inversions. Rather than strumming the chords use the **Chord Pull** technique. For three-string chords use your right hand *thumb* (**p**), *index* (**i**) and *middle* (**m**) finger to pull the notes at the same time. For four-string chords use your right hand *thumb* (**p**), *index* (**i**), *middle* (**m**) and *ring* (**a**) finger to pull the chord.

WHAT IS THE DIFFERENCE BETWEEN A CHORD VOICING, A CHORD SHAPE AND A CHORD INVERSION?

Chord shapes can be played in different places up the neck of the Ukulele. We use the term **"Voicing"** when referring to chord shapes which have a different pitch and tonality. Each chord has a unique sound or *voice*. We choose the sound or *voicing* that works best with the melody and structure of the music.

Chords are made of three or more notes from a 7 note scale. We use a **Chord Formula** for each chord type (Major, Minor ...etc.). The formula to determine the notes for a Major chord is **1- 3 - 5**, or the first (root note), third and fifth note of the scale.

From a **Bb** scale the *Chord Spelling* of a **Bb** chord is: **Bb** (Root 1), **D** (2) and **F** (3). Because the **Bb** is the first note or **Root Note** of the *Chord Spelling* we identify **Bb D F** as the **Root Position** of a **Bb** chord.

If we use the same notes, but change the order of the **Bb Chord Spelling** to **D F Bb**, it is considered the **First Inversion**. Each inversion is considered a different **"voicing"** of the **Bb** chord. In the example to the right we see two **Movable Chord Shapes** used to create different **inversions** or **"voicings "** of the **Bb** Chord.

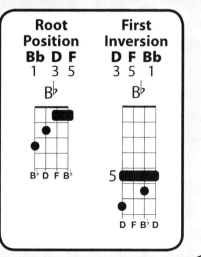

Londonderry Air (Danny Boy)

Traditional

Arranged by KEV

"Londonderry Air" was a traditional Irish melody. Frederic Weatherly modified the lyrics of *"Danny Boy"* to fit the rhyme and meter of *"Londonderry Air"* and the song was later recorded by numerous artists around the world.

Lesson: Practice Playing Barre Chords and Melody

Practice using the **Roman Numeral Position Markers** with the *Chord Pull Technique,* and play the *melody notes* underneath an *Index Finger Barre* as indicated in the notation.

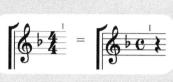

WHY IS THERE A "C" IN ᴛʜᴇ TIME SIGNATURE?

In Western music the most *common time* signature is 4/4. The top number tells us there are 4 beats per measure. The bottom number tells us each beat is a quarter note. The "C" means *Common Time,* which is a term that means 4/4 time.

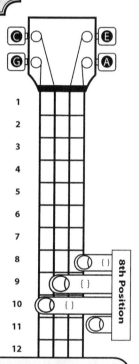

Performance notes:

This song has an **A** and a **B** Section. The **A** section is played in first position. In *measure 11* play the **F7** and reach up to the **D** note on the fifth fret. In section **B** *measures 17 - 23* use the *index* finger of your left hand (fretting hand) to Barre across all 4 strings while you play the melody and chords below it.

In *measures 26 - 27* pay close attention to the **Roman Numeral Position Markers**. In *measure 27* you should be playing in eighth position. Your left (fretting) hand should be at the eighth fret. Use the *ring* finger of your **left** hand to *Barre* across the tenth fret and use your *index* finger to grab the **F** note on the eighth fret.

WHY ARE THE CHORDS ABOVE THE MUSIC SOMETIMES DIFFERENT THAN THE CHORDS IN THE TAB AND MUSIC?

Chords indicated above the music staff are generally used to show the basic chords of a song. In *Fingerstyle Ukulele* we often use chords that include the song's melody note. When you add notes that are not in the basic chord they alter the chord name. In some arrangements they show only the basic chord name and not the altered chord name. For example In *measure* 30 we see a **Dm** indicated above the staff; however, when we include the melody note in the chord it becomes a **Dm7** or an **F6** chord.

Fingerstyle arrangements sometimes show complex chords that add melody notes or additional notes that alter the chords' sound. The arrangement of *"Ah vous dirai-je, Maman"* or *"Twinkle Twinkle Little Star"* is a simple three chord song that was converted into a fingerstyle piece. To make it easier to understand the finger positions, the altered chord diagrams are shown instead of the basic song chords.

Greensleeves

Traditional

Arranged by KEV

"*Greensleeves*" is a traditional English song of unknown origin. It has been attributed to Henry VIII, the much married King of England, with speculation that the words were inspired by Katherine of Aragon or Ann Boleyn. The first mention of the song in recorded history dates around 1580, thirty-three years after the death of Henry VIII.

LESSON: USING WHAT YOU HAVE LEARNED

- *Arpeggio technique*
- *Playing melody notes under an index finger Barre*
- *Chord pulls*
- *Altered Chord Shapes up the neck*

ANACRUSIS. MAKING IT ALL ADD UP.

If every measure in the 6/8 time signature should have six eighth note beats, then why does the first measure have only one eighth note?

An **Anacrusis** is a note or series of *lead-in* notes that come before the first *complete measure* of a composition. It is an introductory (and optional) measure that does not hold the number of beats required by the time signature. The anacrusis prepares your ears for the next measure's downbeat, and is sometimes referred to as the **upbeat**.

Performance notes:

Greensleeves was transcribed in 6/8 time. There are 6 eighth note beats to a measure. When playing this piece use a quick arpeggio technique to add a *"harp-like"* feel to the chord changes.

In *measures 9* and *13* use the **Bb** chord shape pictured to put you into position to play the melody notes after the chord.

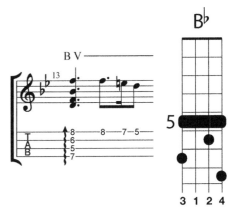

CHORD MELODY -VS- FINGERSTYLE -VS- FINGER PICKING

Chord Melody, in the traditional sense, refers to songs played using mostly chords that contain a melody note. Chord melody songs change chords frequently and use altered chord shapes and inversions to accommodate the melody notes of the song. Chord melody is primarily a rhythmic strumming style of playing used mostly for comping Jazz tunes.

Fingerstyle Ukulele is based on compositions that are focused around a song melody. A fingerstyle arrangement combines the vocal and song melodies with the rhythm and chords of a song. Fingerstyle arrangements can include syncopation, counterpoint, slides, hammer-ons, pull-offs and other techniques and are a preferred style of solo instrumentalists.

Fingerpicking is a word often used interchangeably with the the term Fingerstyle. It is however a term better used to describe a playing style *based on picking patterns*. It is associated with folk songs and often used by songwriters to play a series of fingerpicking patterns over the song's chords. Examples of classic fingerpicking songs: Landslide by Fleetwood Mac, Dust in the Wind by Kansas, The Boxer by Simon and Garfunkel.

Freight Train

Traditional

Arranged by KEV

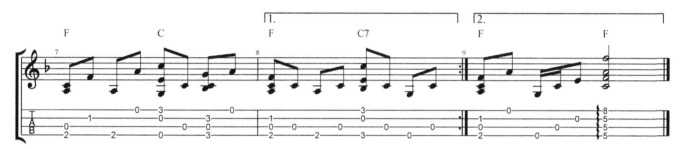

"Freight Train" is a classic American folk song written by Elizabeth Cotten sometime between 1906 and 1912. It was inspired by the sounds of the trains rolling on the tracks near her North Carolina Home.

Lesson: Travis Style Picking and Grace Note Pull-offs

Travis picking is defined by the rhythmic pulse created by alternating between two bass notes. Unlike the guitar, the ukulele does not have two extra bass strings so we must adapt the technique to achieve a similar sound. In this piece we alternate between the **G** (4) string and the **C** (3) string with the thumb and we use our right hand *thumb* (**p**), *index* (**i**) and *middle* (**m**) fingers to grab the melody and notes from the chords to simulate the rhythmic alternating bass feel.

Performance Notes:

The key to Travis style picking is to maintain a consistent beat, like a metronome, while alternating the thumb between strings 4 (**G**) and 3 (**C**) and incorporating the melody and chords without losing the rhythm.

TRAVIS PICKING STYLE

Travis Picking is a term associated with steel string acoustic guitar. It was named after *Merle Travis*, who used a thumb pick to do a rhythmic alternating bass pattern while at the same time comping the melody line. *Chet Atkins* and later the Australian guitarist *Tommy Emmanuel* innovated and popularized this picking style.

GRACE NOTES.

A Grace Note is used in music notation to show musical ornamentation. Grace notes are usually depicted smaller than regular notes to indicate that they are additional non-essential notes to the piece. Typically the grace note is a quick flourish or embellishment that occurs within a beat of music.

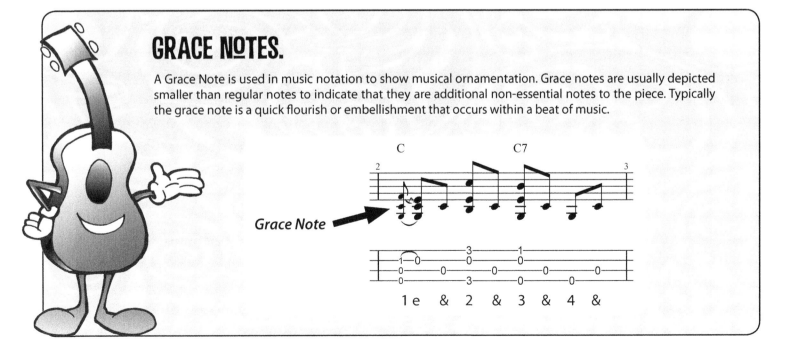

Grace Note

Romance

Anonymous

Arrangement by KEV-Kevin Rones

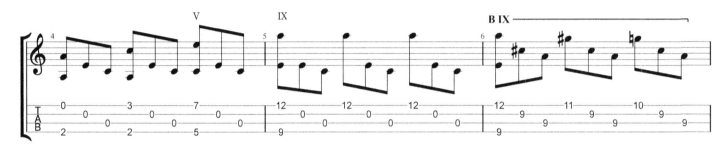

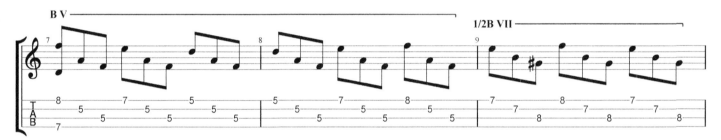

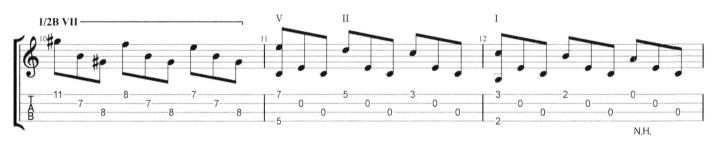

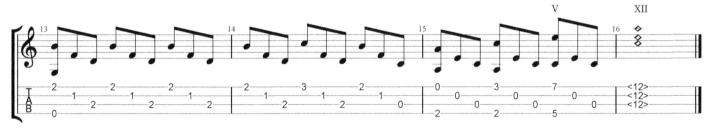

This classical piece is requisite for most classical repertoires. The exact origin of this 19th century piece is unknown. It has been attributed to Francisco Tàrrega and Fernando Sor among others.

Lesson: Classical Picking and Natural Harmonics

Romance, also called *Romanza,* is in **9/8** time. That means you count *nine eighth note beats* per measure. The pulse of this piece is heavier on the first, fourth and seventh note. **1** 2 3 **4** 5 6 **7** 8 9. Pay attention to the **Roman Numeral Position Markers** and the **Barre indicators.**

Performance notes:

You may find this piece difficult to play, particularly if you are playing a soprano sized ukulele. As you move higher up the neck (in pitch) the frets become increasingly smaller.

In *measures 9* and *10* use a **1/2 barre** across the first two strings so you can pivot back and forth and reach up to the 11th fret with your pinkie.

A multi-string **Natural Harmonic** occurs in the last measure and "rings" out for four beats - or until it fades out.

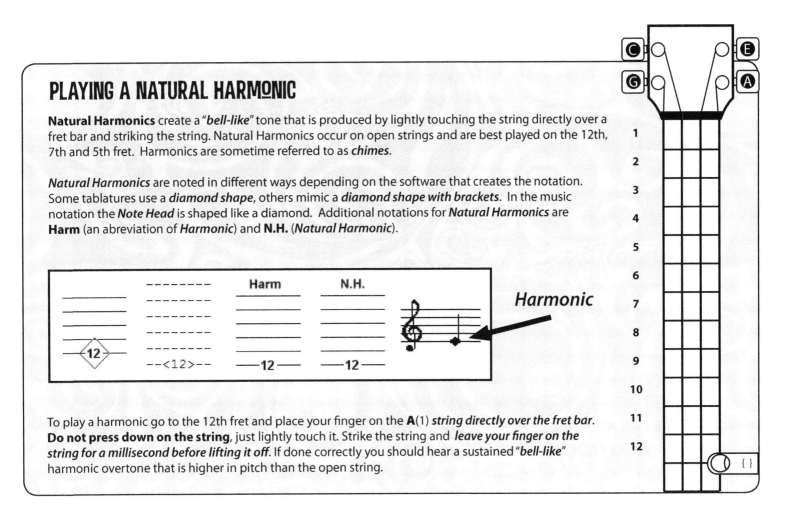

PLAYING A NATURAL HARMONIC

Natural Harmonics create a *"bell-like"* tone that is produced by lightly touching the string directly over a fret bar and striking the string. Natural Harmonics occur on open strings and are best played on the 12th, 7th and 5th fret. Harmonics are sometime referred to as *chimes*.

Natural Harmonics are noted in different ways depending on the software that creates the notation. Some tablatures use a *diamond shape*, others mimic a *diamond shape with brackets*. In the music notation the *Note Head* is shaped like a diamond. Additional notations for *Natural Harmonics* are **Harm** (an abreviation of *Harmonic*) and **N.H.** (*Natural Harmonic*).

To play a harmonic go to the 12th fret and place your finger on the **A**(1) *string directly over the fret bar*. **Do not press down on the string**, just lightly touch it. Strike the string and *leave your finger on the string for a millisecond before lifting it off*. If done correctly you should hear a sustained *"bell-like"* harmonic overtone that is higher in pitch than the open string.

A TRICK FOR DOING HARMONICS

You can do harmonics across multiple strings. A trick for getting the harmonics to ring out more clearly is to strike the strings with the back of the fingernail of the right hand.

Study In Bm

Fernando Sor

Arranged By KEV

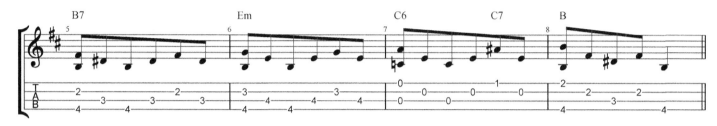

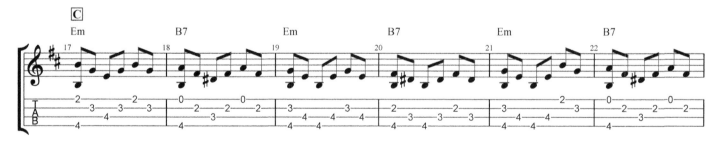

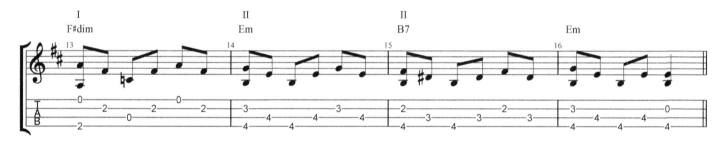

Fernando Sor (1778 – 1839) was a Spanish classical guitarist and composer best known for his guitar compositions, which ranged from guitar pieces for beginning players to advanced players. Sor's contemporaries considered him to be the best guitarist in the world.

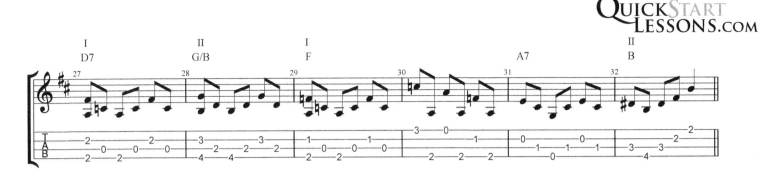

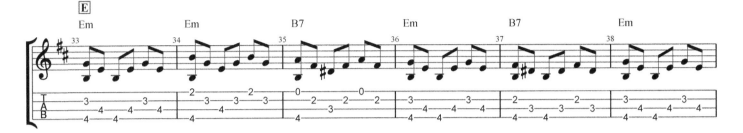

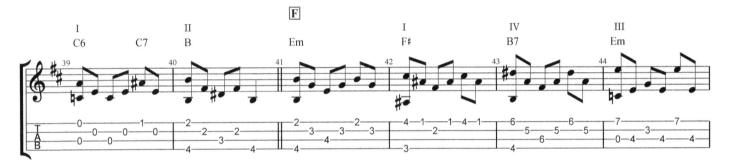

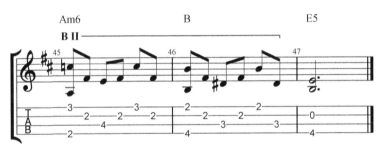

Lesson: Picking Patterns Based Off Chords

This piece uses **picking patterns over chords**. We often "modify" picking patterns when playing over different chord shapes and inversions to get the notes that are harmonically necessary for the piece.

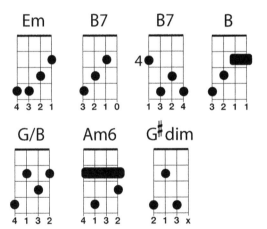

Performance notes:

If you examine the notes for each chord in a measure you can figure out the chord shapes. For example *Measures 1-6* alternate between a closed position **Em** and an open position **B7**.

Start *measure 42* in first position with your pinkie on the fourth fret of the **A** (1) string and ring finger on the third fret of the **G** (4) string. In *measure 44* anchor your pinkie on the seventh fret of the **A** (1) string for the duration of the measure.

D7 OR NOT D7...THAT IS THE QUESTION.

The **D7 chord** pictured in the middle has no **D** note in it. It is technically an **F# diminished** chord. We commonly call this the *Easy D7*. It could more precisely be called a **D7 with no root**.

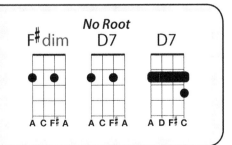

Dance of the Galway Pixie

Original

by KEV

Lesson: Using the Claw Technique

The **Claw Technique** is done by using a combination of your right hand thumb, index and middle fingers to grab three-string combinations. Your *Index (i)* and *Middle (m)* fingers stay together as if they were fused to each other to form a Claw. The technique allows you to use use your index and middle fingers as a tool to play two strings simultaneously while freeing up the thumb to do other things. This technique is used often when playing fingerstyle pieces.

Performance notes:

This exersong™ uses the *Claw Technique* to play the bass note with the thumb, and the Claw fingers to alternate between different string sets. The bridge section incorporates *Slides*, *Hammer-ons* and *Arpeggiated chord techniques*.

The Claw

CHECK YOUR HAND POSITION

If you look at down at your hand position your fingers should make an **X** shape. This is the correct form for fingerpicking. Note: The Thumb is *ABOVE* the fingers.

UNDERSTANDING THE SLIDE FROM NOWHERE.

In *measure 13* we see a slide that ends on the **D** note of the fifth fret... but it has no starting note. This means you *slide into the fifth fret*. The best way to play this is to *press down as you start your slide one or two frets* away and stop at the indicated fret.

The Slide from nowhere

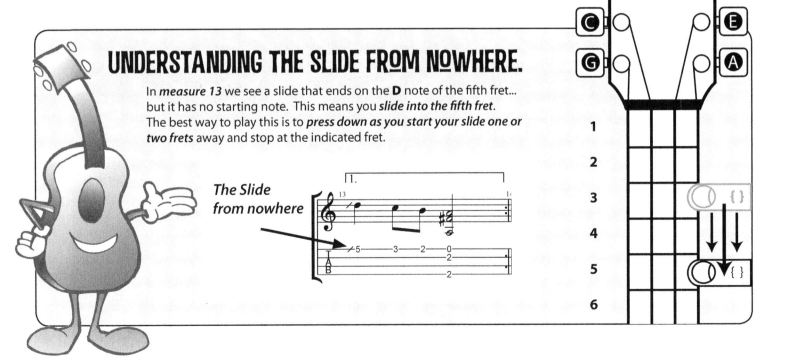

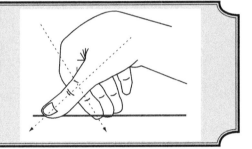

The Cowpokes Dream

Original

Music by KEV

Lesson: Dynamic Markings

There are two examples of dynamic notation in this exersong™. Each serves a different purpose.

mf **Mezzo-forte** (pronounced met'-so FOR-tay) is an Italian term literally translating as *half loud*. In music notation *mezzo-forte* (Moderately loud) is considered softer than **forte** (loud). If no dynamic notation is indicated then *mezzo-forte* is assumed to be the the starting dynamic level. This type of dynamic notation sets the starting volume for the piece and is found in the *first measure* of music. If the "feel" of the piece changes in volume or intensity, additional volume notation is used.

> The **Accent Symbol** seen directly under the first note on the music staff of this piece is the notation symbol for an *accent*. When the accent symbol is present you add emphasis to that note or series of notes by playing them louder than the other notes in the piece. This mark is correctly known by classically trained musicians as a **marcato**, this is Italian for "*well marked*" though it is usually simply referred to as an accent.

Performance notes:

It's a good idea to use a *base dynamic sound level* that allows you the ability to play louder or softer in a piece. In this exersong™ we use the accents to give the feeling of two different parts being played simultaneously. In *measure 13* we use a series if *hammer-ons* and *pull-offs*.

DYNAMIC NOTATION SYMBOLS

Term	Sign	Meaning
piano	*p*	quiet
mezzo piano	*mp*	moderately quiet
pianissimo	*pp*	very quiet
forte	*f*	loud
mezzo forte	*mf*	moderately loud
fortissimo	*ff*	very loud
subito forte	*sf*	suddenly loud
subito forte piano	*sfp*	suddenly loud and soft
sforzando	*sfz*	forceful sudden accent

SOMETIMES THE MUSIC CALLS FOR THE VOLUME TO SWELL OR DIMINISH.

These *Italian words* are used to indicate gradual changes in volume.

- **crescendo** (abbreviated **cresc.**) translates as "increasing" (literally "growing").
- **decrescendo** (abbreviated to **decresc.**) translates as *decreasing*.
- **diminuendo** (abbreviated **dim.**) translates as *diminishing*.

Angled line symbols, sometimes referred to as *"Hairpins"* are used as a visual notation to show how long the music swells or decreases. *Hairpins* are usually written below the staff (or between the two staves in a grand staff).

THE IMPORTANCE OF DYNAMICS

Dynamics and the ability to use them effectively are one of the differences between a *great player* and a *mediocre player*. Dynamics are a way to create interest and to add emotion to a piece. The ukulele has a limited dynamic range, so we have to use every tool at our disposal to get the most dynamic range possible.

Dynamics are created by *increasing* or *decreasing* the *volume and intensity of the attack* of a note or group of notes within a passage. There is no set "volume" for dynamic markings. The markings are relative to each other and the volume the performer starts with sets the dynamic level for the piece. Every performance and venue are different.

By using dynamics you can create a more interesting experience for your audience. Dynamics draw the listeners in and keep them listening.

March Of The Wind-up Robots

Original

By KEV

Lesson 16 : Chromatic Runs and Adding Dynamics to Chords

This exersong™ is in 2/4 time. Each measure gets 2 quarter note beats of music. Count the eighth notes in this piece like this: **1** & **2** & **1** & **2** &. There are dynamic accents featuring chords, arpeggiated chords, some chromatic note runs and phrases.

Performance notes:

On the chords with an accent symbol use a quicker attack using the nail on the back of your *index* (**i**) finger. Pay attention to which chords are accented and which chords are arpeggiated. Practice using the *Walking Fingers* technique, using alternating *index* (**i**) and *middle* (**m**)fingers, on the chromatic runs and phrases.

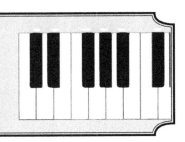

WHAT IS A CHROMATIC RUN?

A **Chromatic Run** on a piano means playing every note (all black and white keys) either *ascending* or *descending* from the starting note. On ukulele every fret is a half step, so you play every fret in the order of pitch, and when switching to another string start on the fret corresponding to the next half step pitch.

Gypsy Dance

Original

Music by KEV

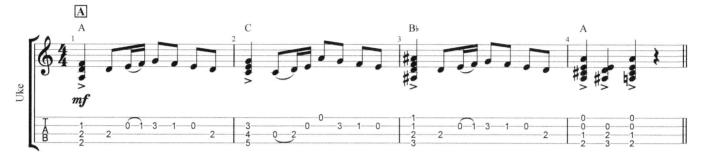

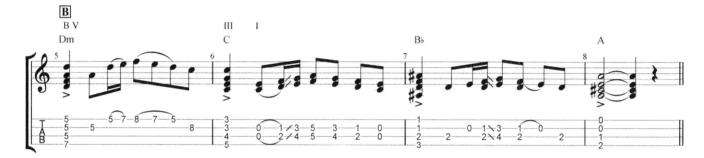

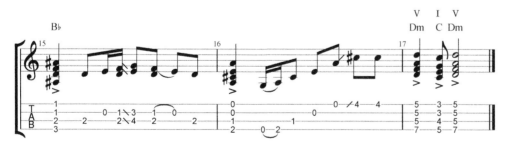

HOW TO PULL OFF A MULTIPLE PULL-OFF

B
B V
Dm

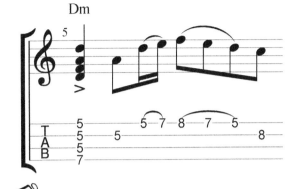

MULTIPLE PULL-OFFS: THREE NOTES FOR THE PRICE OF ONE PLUCK!

In this example we see an *accented* **Dm** Chord followed by a *Hammer-on* from *fret 5* to *fret 7* and a **Multiple Pull-off** using *Frets 8, 7* and *5*. Notation for a **Multiple Pull-off** looks similar to an umbrella over 3 or more notes.

Anchor the *index finger* of your fretting hand on the *fifth fret* of the **A** (1) string and directly below, on the same string, anchor your *ring finger* on the *seventh fret*. Then place your *pinkie* on the eighth fret. *You should now have three fingers* on the **A**(1) string on *frets 5, 7* and *8*.
Strike the string and pull-off the *pinkie* while still anchoring the *ring* and *index fingers*. Then immediately *pull-off* the *ring* finger to hear the sound of the **D** note on the *fifth fret*. With this technique you hear *all three notes with one pluck*.

A PLETHORA OF PICKING TECHNIQUES

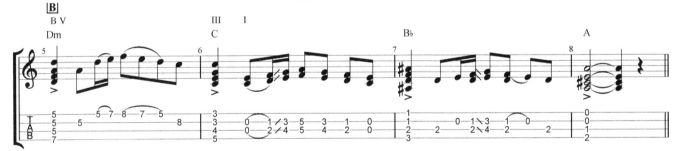

This exersong™ is chock-full of technique. In this example from *measure 5* you see an *Accented Chord, Hammer-on* and a *Multiple Pull-off*. In *measure 6* you see a *Double Hammer-on* that moves into a *Slide*, and a *Run of Thirds*. In *measure 7* you see *Double Slide* followed by a *Double Pluck with a single Pull-off*.

PLAYING THIRDS

The sound of thirds is often associated with the ukulele. The correct technique for playing thirds, shown in the illustration to the right, is to use a **Slant Position** and a **Parallel Position**. Use the *index* and *middle* finger for the slant. For the *Parallel Position* pivot, leading with your middle finger. Use your ring finger to fret the second note.

Note: If you play a Slant *higher up the neck* after a parallel, be consistent; change position and use the correct fingers!

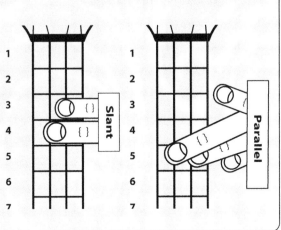

The Road To Lothlorien
Original

Music by KEV

Lesson: Incorporating Hammer-ons and Pull-offs into a Picking Pattern

You can add interest to your playing by adding **Hammer-ons** and **Pull-offs** into your picking patterns. This exersong™ incorporates **Hammer-ons** and **Pull-offs** into two different picking patterns.

Performance notes:

This piece is all done in **First Position**. In *measure 1* use the *middle finger* of your fretting hand to hammer down on the **second fret** of the the **C (3)** string and keep it there. After the *Hammer-on* play the **F** note on the first fret of the **E (2)** string and keep it there. This sets you up to use your *ring* finger to *pull-off* from the third fret to the first fret.

In measure 3 stay in **First Position**. Start with your middle finger on the second fret of the the **G (4)** string and *Hammer-on* with the ring finger. Then move your middle finger to the second fret of the **C (3)** string and hold it there to the end of the measure.

I Love Kona

Original

Music by KEV

Lesson: Adding Pinch, Pulls and Slides into a Picking Pattern

In *measure 1* we use a **Two String Pinch with a Hammer-on**. To do this technique form an **F** chord, then lift up your *middle finger*. Pinch *strings 2* and *4* together, and after you release the pluck, hammer down with your *middle finger* on the second fret of the **G (4)** string.

In *measure 5* we use a **Chord Pull** with a **Hammer-On**. This is a quick hammer-on used as an ornamentation. Form the chord shape and lift off your *middle finger*. Use your **Thumb and Claw** to pull the three strings and a millisecond after you release the pull, hammer down with your *middle finger* on the second fret of the **C** (4) string.

In *measure 4* start in **First Position**. Use your *ring finger* to slide from the third fret to the fifth fret. That moves you into **Third Position**. Use your fretting hand index finger to to play the **C** note on the third fret of the **A** (1) string, then slide back from the fifth fret to the third fret with your *ring finger*. You should then be back in *First Position*.

In *measure 9* form the first chord shape and keep it there until the **Multiple Pull-off** in *measure 11*. Reach up wth your *pinkie* in *measure 10* to reach the notes on the fifth and sixth frets

Performance notes:

This exersong™ is jam-packed with techniques. Practice adding **Hammer-ons**, **Pull-offs** and **Slides** to augment your picking patterns.

Ukulele Breakdown 2

Original

Music by KEV

THE BANJOLELE

The **Banjolele** or **Banjo Uke** was first created around 1917. It has the smaller scale, the tuning of a ukulele and the tone of a banjo. Banjoleles became popular in the 1920's and 1930's with vaudeville performers who wanted an instrument with the size and ease of play of the ukulele, but with more volume.

The Banjolele was popularized by the British comedian George Formby (1904–1961), who developed his own style of playing in accompaniment to his comic songs.

HOW TO PLAY A BANJO ROLL

1. Start in **Third Position**. Anchor your *index* finger of your left hand on the third fret of the **C** (3) string

2. Grab strings 3, 2 & 1 using your *right hand thumb* (**p**) on string 3, index (**i**) on string 2 and middle (**m**) finger on string 1 (*your right thumb should be above the plucking fingers*).

3. Pull all three strings as you **hammer down** with your *middle finger* on fret four of the **C** (3) string (and keep it there) and then strike the **C** (3) string again with a downward motion of your thumb (**p**) and quickly kick up with your middle finger to strike the **A** (1) string.

4. With the hammer *still* down on the fourth fret of the **C** (3) string, strike downward again on string 3 with your *thumb* (**p**) and strike up on the **E** (2) string with your index (**i**)

5. Strike downward again on the **C** (3) string with your thumb (**p**) and quickly kick up with your middle finger to strike the **A** (1) string again.

TAKING A CLOSER LOOK AT THE TECHNIQUE: FANCY SHMANCY END TAG

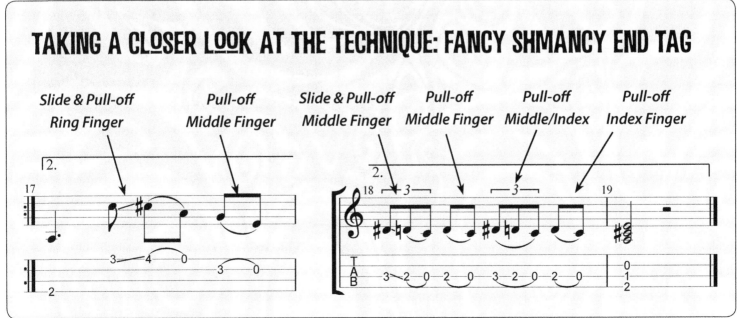

40

Lesson: Broke Neck Chicken Clawhammer Technique

Clawhammer technique comes from American old-time banjo music. It is sometimes referred to as *Frailing*. *Clawhammer technique* can be used to create rhythmic percussive effects by brushing or thumping the thumb or fingers on the strings.

Clawhammer picking is primarily a down-picking style. Only the thumb and middle and/or index finger are used. The strumming hand forms a *"claw"* with the thumb, index and middle finger. Downward strums are done with the index and/or middle finger by hitting the string with the back of the fingernail.

Performance notes:

A clawhammer purist would use only downstrokes; however, for this exersong™ we have added some additional techniques and a fun ending lick to impress your friends and neighbors.

Use your thumb to play single notes on the fourth string **G (4)**. Note that the arrows in the first measure of the tablature (tab) point upward. In tab this means you strum down from the low string to the high string. Keep your strumming hand relaxed and create a strumming motion by moving your arm from the elbow joint in a rocking motion and strumming a downward brush with the back of the fingernails. Keep a steady rhythm.

In *measure 7* there are a series of *hammer-ons* and a *slide*. Normally you would alternate your right hand picking using the thumb (**p**) in a downward motion on the **G (4)** string and the *index* (**i**) in an upward motion on the **C (3)** string. However you can choose to strike the **C (3)** string with the back of your *index* (**i**) nail in a downward motion if you want to play more traditionally.

In *measures* 10 and 11 there are *slides* using 6ths. Use your picking hand *thumb* (**p**) and *middle* (**m**) to pick them. To play the ending lick in *measures 13* and *14* barre across the seventh fret with your fretting hand index finger and alternate the picking between your *thumb* (**p**) and *index* (**i**) finger.

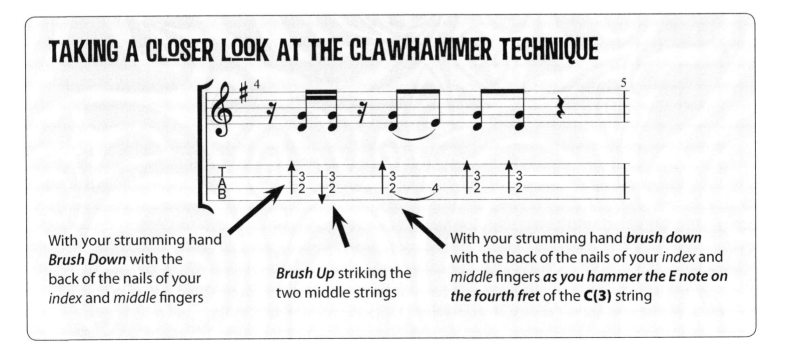

TAKING A CLOSER LOOK AT THE CLAWHAMMER TECHNIQUE

With your strumming hand **Brush Down** with the back of the nails of your *index* and *middle* fingers

Brush Up striking the two middle strings

With your strumming hand **brush down** with the back of the nails of your *index* and *middle* fingers *as you hammer the E note on the fourth fret* of the **C(3)** string

ABOUT THE AUTHOR

KEV - *Kevin Rones* is a San Diego based ukulele player, author, educator and acoustic performer. He has written several CenterStream/Hal Leonard instruction books including *Ukulele 101, Kid's Ukulele Activity Book, Fingerstyle Ukulele, Fingerstyle Ukulele 2, and Blues Ukulele.*

His fun hands-on teaching method and energetic performances make him a popular teacher and performer at Ukulele Festivals, Concerts and Music Camps.

He is a **Kala Brand Ukulele Artist** and a **Taylor Guitar Artist**, and has been top competitor in the International Fingerstyle guitar championships.

He is the founder of the *Sneaky Tiki Ukulele Meetup & Social Club, the Awesome Uke YouTube channel,* the *San Diego Ukulele Orchestra program,* and is currently working on *QuickStartLessons on Demand,* an online education site for the ukulele.

WHERE DO YOU GO FROM HERE? *Three things you can do now.*

1. Check out Kev's other **QuickStart Ukulele books** available at www.HalLeonard.com, BarnesAndNoble.com, Amazon.com, GuitarCenter and quality music stores everywhere.

2. Subscribe to KEV's *Awesome Uke YouTube channel.*

3. *Go online to get bonus content, bonus videos created specifically for this book, and downloadable ukulele resources.*

GET FREE UKE STUFF. JOIN THE TIKI NATION

It's the membership site about everything ukulele!
Ukulele Podcasts, Video Lessons, Downloads & More!

TheTikiNation.com

To access audio files for Fingerstyle Ukulele 2 visit: **www.HalLeonard.com/QuickStartLessonsLibrary** and enter the code printed on the title page of this book

THANK YOU FOR PUCHASING THIS BOOK.

Without the support of the ukulele community the *QuickStartlessons™ series* of Ukulele instructional books would not be possible. Our goal is to create fun, useful, hands-on instructional material that is presented in an easy to understand method.

If you don't see our *QuickStartLessons books* or our *Learn & Play series* in your local retail music store please ask them to order them from **www.HalLeonard.com**.

SPECIAL THANKS!

Thanks to the nice folks at *Kala Brand Music Co.* for their continued support.

New to ukulele?
KEV recommends and plays Kala Brand Ukuleles.

CHECK OUT THESE QUICKSTART UKULELE BOOKS

QUICKSTART FINGERSTYLE UKULELE
For Soprano, Concert or Tenor Ukuleles in Standard C Tuning (High G)

Combining picking patterns, chord strumming & melody lines for interesting and fun arrangements, fingerstyle ukulele has become popular with indie artists and emerging solo uke players around the world. This new book will help anyone move beyond three chords and a strum! Kev covers techniques and patterns, tablature, music reading and much more, with arrangements written specifically for fingerstyle uke in styles ranging from Celtic to classical! Perfect for uke newbies, guitarists ready to take on a new instrument, and singer-songwriters looking to expand their horizons.
$17.99   Item Number: HL.1590   ISBN 1574242784   9x12 inches

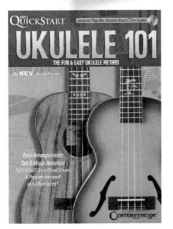

UKULELE 101: THE FUN & EASY UKULELE METHOD

Thinking about playing the ukulele? This book is an excellent introduction to the world of the ukulele. With the method presented here, you can gain a basic understanding of the instrument, and amaze & impress your friends and family with your new knowledge and playing abilities! Many of the Exersongs™ in this book are done in tablature and standard music notation with chords so you can practice strumming, or play the melody and picking patterns along with the music tracks. *Get started on the ukulele today!*
$17.99   Item Number: HL.119896   ISBN 157424292X   9x12 inches

KID'S UKE - UKULELE ACTIVITY FUN BOOK
Learn & Play Series

Get your kids involved and excited about music with this fun **Learn & Play Kid's Activity Book.** It's the perfect introduction to the ukulele for kids. Learn about the ukulele and how to play it through a series of fun projects including songs, coloring, note reading, puzzles, crosswords, a word search, chords and more.
$11.99   Item Number: HL.173015   ISBN 1574243314   9x12 inches

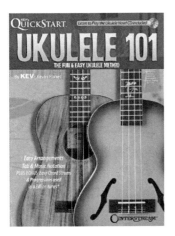

QUICKSTART UKULELE BLUES: LICKS, TRICKS & MORE
The Ukulele Player's Guide to the Blues

This book is designed as a guide to help you learn to play & jam to the blues. The method presented in this book will enable you to gain a basic understanding of blues ukulele to amaze and impress your friends, family, and even your dog with your new knowledge and playing abilities! Written in standard music notation and tablature, you'll learn blues form, 12-bar blues, blues shuffle rhythm, 8-bar blues shuffle, the secret method of jamming, how to bend the notes, blues scales in different keys, minor blues, blues songs, bonus jam trax and much more. This book will have you playing blues in no time!
$19.99   Item Number: HL.141051   ISBN 1574243128   9x12 inches

More Great Ukulele Books from Centerstream...